SMART ABOUT
Art

FRIDA KAHLO

The Artist Who Painted Herself

by
Frieda Fry

Written by Margaret Frith
Illustrated by Tomie dePaola

Grosset & Dunlap · New York

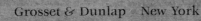

For Tomie who introduced me
to Frida—Mgt

For Margaret Frith
who doesn't have eyebrows like a bird
and Mario who does—TdeP

Front cover: *The Frame, Self-Portrait*,1937. © CNAC/MNAM/Dist. Reunion des Musees Nationaux/Art Resource, NY.

All artwork by Frida Kahlo copyright © 2003 Banco de Mexico Diego Rivera and Frida Kahlo Museum Trust, Av. Cinco de Mayo No.2, Col. Centro, Del. Cuauhtemoc 06059, Mexico, D.F.

Text copyright © 2003 by Margaret Frith. Illustrations copyright © 2003 by Tomie dePaola. All rights reserved. Published by Grosset & Dunlap, a division of Penguin Young Readers Group, 345 Hudson Street, New York, NY 10014. GROSSET & DUNLAP is a trademark of Penguin Group (USA) Inc. Published simultaneously in Canada. Manufactured in China.

Library of Congress Cataloging-in-Publication Data is available.

ISBN 0-448-42677-3 (pbk)   A B C D E F G H I J
ISBN 0-448-43239-0 (GB)   A B C D E F G H I J

From the desk of
Ms. Brandt

Dear Class,

Our unit on famous artists is almost over. I hope that you enjoyed it as much as I did.

I am excited to read your reports. Here are some questions that you may want to think about:

- Why did you pick your artist?

- If you could ask your artist 3 questions, what would they be?

- Did you learn anything that really surprised you?

Good luck and have fun!

Ms. Brandt

Self-Portrait as a Tehuana (Diego on my Mind), 1943. © Rafael Doniz.

This costume was one of Frida's favorites.

My name is Frieda. It's not an ordinary name and when I found out that there was an artist named Frida, I picked her for my report. Her full name is Frida Kahlo. She spells her name with an "i." I use an "ie."

I love to dress up. So did Frida. I know this because of all the pictures she painted of herself. She always wore fancy clothes with long skirts. (I'll tell you why later.) The painting on the opposite page is one of her fanciest pictures. She even painted a tiny picture of her husband right on her forehead. Weird!

Kahlo rhymes with follow.

This is me dressing up like Frida.

pretze[l]
braid

weird
necklace

Self-Portrait with Braid, 1941. © Rafael Doniz.

Frida never smiled in her paintings. (I read that it was
because she had bad teeth.) She liked to paint her
eyebrows to look like the wings of a bird.

Frida Kahlo is from Mexico. She is Mexico's most famous woman artist. The paintings she did of herself are called self-portraits. She put bright-colored ribbons and flowers through her thick black braids. She wore earrings and necklaces made of jade and silver. She wore tons of rings on her fingers.

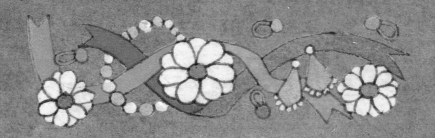

This is Frida's family tree.

My Grandparents, My Parents, and I (Family Tree),1936. Digital Image copyright The Museum of Modern Art/Licensed by SCALA/Art Resource, NY.

Frida was born in Mexico on July 6, 1907. Her mother was from Mexico. Her father came from Germany. He was a photographer. She had three sisters, but she was her father's favorite. He said, "She's the most like me." I think that when Frida grew up, she looked a lot like her grandma on her father's side. She's at the top right of the picture.

The family lived in a small town near Mexico City. They called their house the *Casa Azul*. That's Spanish for Blue House. Frida painted herself as a little girl standing in the courtyard of the Blue House. She uses a red ribbon to tie herself to her family.

Dad's parents

Mom's parents

My parents

The Frys
Pierre and Jeanne
Paris, France

The Carrs
Norman and Frieda
London, England

Marc and Elizabeth
U.S.A.

Me

This is my family tree. People say that I look like Grandpa Pierre. (Only I don't have a beard!)

When Frida was six, she got very sick. She had a disease called polio. She couldn't walk, and she had to stay in bed for almost a year. She was by herself a lot. She made up a pretend friend. The friend didn't speak, but she laughed and danced and Frida told her all her secrets.

When Frida was better, her right leg was very thin. Her father made her ride a bicycle and swim. But her leg was still thin. At school kids teased her. They called her Frida *pato a palo*, Frida "peg leg." Frida wore long skirts to hide her leg.

Frida went to another school when she was fifteen. She met new friends. They called themselves "The Caps" for the red caps they wore. They liked Frida because she was funny and did crazy things. Once a famous painter was at the school working on a big picture that he was painting on a wall. (This kind of painting is called a mural.) He was a big man. Frida rubbed soap on the steps where he walked every day. She hoped he would slip and fall down like a clown. But he didn't. His name was Diego Rivera.

Frida's red cap

Frida was eighteen when she was badly hurt in a terrible bus accident. She had to stay in bed again for a long time.

Frida had never thought about painting. She thought she might be a doctor. One day her mother gave her some paints and brushes and put a big mirror in the canopy over the bed. Frida could look up and see her face. She started to paint pictures of herself.

Frida stayed at home for two years. She painted over twenty-four paintings of herself, her sisters, and her friends.

When Frida got better, she took four of the paintings to Diego Rivera. She didn't really know him, but she remembered him painting that big picture at her school. She found him and there he was still painting big pictures up on walls.

Frida called up to him, "Diego, come down!" And he did! I think she was so brave to do that.

Diego looked at her paintings. He said he liked the one of her in a velvet dress.

"It's original," he said. He meant that she hadn't copied another artist's way of doing a painting. He told her to go home and do another painting. He would go to her house the next Sunday and look at it.

Frida and Diego on their wedding day

Frida and Diego at home, Coyoacan, Mexico, 1941. © Emmy Lou Packard. Courtesy of Throckmorton Fine Art, New York.

He did and two years after that, Frida and Diego got married. I wonder if he ever knew that she was the girl who soaped the steps!

Frida's father called them "the elephant and the dove." Maybe that's why she put a dove in her painting.

Here's the dove.

Frida and Diego Rivera, 1931. Oil on canvas, 39 3/8 in x 31 in. San Francisco Museum of Modern Art. Albert M. Bender Collection, Gift of Albert M. Bender © Estate of Frida Kahlo, Courtesy Banco de Mexico.

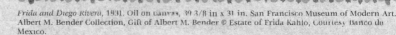

San Francisco

I wonder why
she painted
him next to
a boat.

Portrait of Dr. Eloesser, 1931. University of California, San Francisco School of Medicine.

Frida and Diego went to San Francisco. Diego
had a job working on murals. Frida met new people
and she painted some of them. A man named Dr. Leo
Eloesser became her doctor and her good friend.

Sometimes Frida's paintings look like weird dreams. But Frida said, "I never painted dreams." She said she just painted what she saw. I think she meant what she saw in her imagination.

At first, the painting below looks very strange. But it is of a scientist named Luther Burbank. He was famous for growing new kinds of plants. So it makes sense that Mr. Burbank is in a painting with lots of trees.

Portrait of Luther Burbank, 1931. Copyright Schalkwijk/Art Resource, NY.

I wonder if Mr. Burbank liked seeing himself coming out of a tree.

Frida and Diego left San Francisco and went to New York and Detroit. Frida really missed home. In New York she painted *My Dress Hangs Here*. She is not wearing the dress, so where is she? Maybe she is wishing she were back in Mexico.

After three years, Frida and Diego finally took a boat home.

Statue of Liberty

New York City skyscrapers

This is Mae West.

She was a big movie star.

My Dress Hangs Here, 1933–1938. Christie's Images/Superstock.

Frida and Diego still went on trips to visit other countries.

Once Frida went to Paris and met the famous painter Pablo Picasso. He taught her songs and gave her clay earrings in the shape of hands, one for each ear.

See the hand earring.

Self-Portrait Dedicated to Dr. Eloesser, 1940 Mary-Anne Martin/Fine Art, New York.

Paris, France

This is a picture of Frida's Blue House and garden.

In 1941 Frida and Diego moved to the Blue House where Frida was born. They painted the front of the house a really deep blue that in Spanish is called *azul anil*. (This was supposed to keep out evil spirits.) They added green and red around the doors and windows. I think it is a really pretty house.

She grew lots of plants and flowers such as marguerites, mimosas, and jasmines. She kept parrots, songbirds, parakeets, cats, dogs, monkeys, and a little deer called Granizo. They were all over the courtyard and in the garden. I wish I could go to Mexico and see the Blue House. It is still there and you can visit it.

Frida loved living in the Blue House with Diego.
She cooked. She laughed. Friends and family came to
eat. They all talked. They argued. They sang until it
was late at night. And Frida painted in the studio that
Diego built for her.

Frida and Diego in Blue House, 1941. Courtesy of Throckmorton Fine Art, New York.

Frida loved to dress up her dining room table just
like she loved to dress up herself. She put flowers in
her hair to match the ones on the table. Or she wore
a necklace made of the flowers from the table. She
liked mimosas and marguerites a lot.

Frida collected things from all over Mexico. She bought toys and dolls to add to the ones she had as a child. She put them in the Blue House.

She especially liked figures made out of papier-mâché. (Papier-mâché is paper that you mix with a wet mixture until it gets mushy. Then you can shape it into whatever you want and when it dries it is hard like a rock.) I read that she even had a papier-mâché skeleton as big as a person hanging next to her bed.

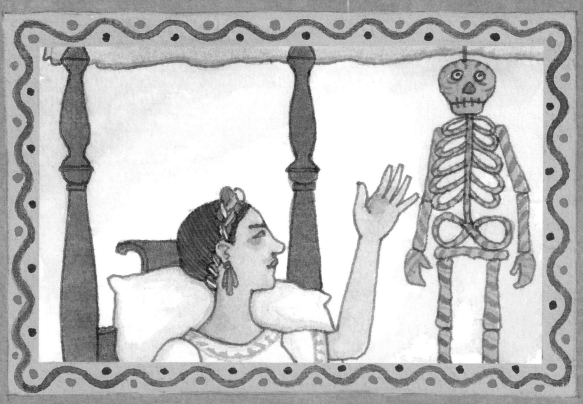

Every morning she would wake up and say, "¡Hola, mana!"
That means, "Hi there, sis!"

Frida loved holidays, especially a Mexican holiday called the Day of the Dead. It takes place on two days, November 1 and 2. It sounds like a sad holiday, but it's not. It is a happy time to remember family and friends who have died.

Every year Frida decorated a table with candles and golden flowers. Then she put all of her mother and father's favorite foods on the table, along with little sugar skulls and sugar animals—lambs, chickens, and ducks. There were also small dancing skeletons made out of papier-mâché.

It sounds as if Frida was always having a good time. But she wasn't. Ever since the bus accident, she was in pain. She had thirty-two operations and she had to wear a brace or a corset most of her life. That's probably why she kept on wearing those long skirts.

Frida was grateful to her doctors for taking care of her. Once she wrote in her diary: "Dr. Farill saved me. He brought me the joy of living."

Here is a picture she painted of herself sitting in her wheelchair painting her doctor.

Self-Portrait with Portrait of Dr. Juan Farill, 1951. Mary-Anne Martin/Fine Art, New York.

Frida made the wooden palette look like a real heart.

Frida kept an interesting diary. She drew all over the pages. Some of her drawings are so strange I can't even tell what they are. And she didn't just write in it like most people do. She used colored pencils, pens, and watercolors and the colors she used matched what she was writing about. Red, yellow, green, and brown writing are all over the pages along with her sketches.

This is a page from my diary the way Frida might have written it.

Dear Diary,

We went to the zoo today on our class trip. I saw lots of animals just like the ones Frida had in her garden—

❀ spider monkeys

❀ a fawn (that's a little deer)

❀ parrots (Frida's parrots probably spoke Spanish!)

Sometimes Frida put her animals in her paintings. (I'm going to put my cat in my next painting.)

A big thing happened to Frida in 1953. It is very special to have your paintings and no one else's in a show. Frida was the first woman artist in Mexico to have her own show.

The first night is called the "opening." She really wanted to be there, but she was too sick to walk or use her wheelchair. So they put her four-poster bed in the middle of the room and carried her in on a stretcher.

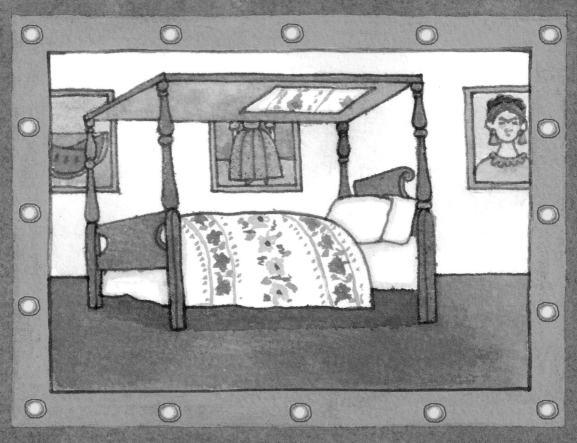

Frida went home at the end of the opening, but they kept her bed in the show.

Frida was so brave. She never gave up. Even when she had to stay in bed, she kept painting and dressing in her wonderful clothes. She wore her jewelry and braided her hair in ribbons or flowers. She always looked just like a painting.

Frida Kahlo reclining on her bed, Coyoacan, Mexico (ca.1942–1945). Chester Dale Papers 1897–1971, Archives of American Art, Smithsonian Institution.

Frida kept tons of photographs of family and friends on her bed.

I wish that Frida wasn't smoking!

I like Frida's paintings a lot. I am proud to
have the same name. So many of her paintings
are of herself. Still they are all different. Some make
me feel sad. Some make me laugh. Some make me
wonder where she got her ideas because they are
so strange—like this one. You can't stop looking at it,
even though it's kind of scary.

The Two Fridas, 1939. Copyright Schalkwijk/Art Resource, NY.

But not this one! Juicy red watermelons with bright green skins. It was one of the last paintings Frida did. She was just forty-seven years old when she died in 1954.

It's my favorite because of what she wrote on the watermelon.

Viva la Vida! That means Long Live Life!

I say VIVA LA FRIDA!

If I met Frida I would ask her:

Why didn't you ever smile in your paintings?
Was it really hard to paint lying down?
Why did you paint two Fridas in one picture?

Frieda,
   I saw a movie about
Frida, but I learned
many new things from
your report. You did a
wonderful job showing
why Frida Kahlo painted
so many self-portraits.
   Thank you and ....

Viva la Frieda!

Ms. Brandt

Frida's on
a U. S. stamp.